Publishing

In CHARGE
of My Life

Delila Vasquez
(transcribed by Crystal Sapir)

from *Empower Publishing*

In CHARGE of My Life

Delila Vasquez

Transcribed by: Crystal Sapir, Teacher of
DeafBlind

Empower Publishing
Winston-Salem

Empower

Publishing

Empower Publishing
302 Ricks Drive
Winston-Salem, NC 27103

First Empower Publishing Books edition published
April, 2023
Empower Publishing, Feather Pen, and all production design are trademarks.

For information regarding bulk purchases of this book, digital purchase and special discounts, please contact the publisher at publish.empower.now@gmail.com

Cover design by Melissa Brito, Dallas Museum of Art

Manufactured in the United States of America
ISBN 978-1-63066-562-3

Foreword:
A Note From My Mom:

"You talked back, you did numerous mischievous things that would get you into trouble, you are strong minded and once something is on your mind you don't give up. It drives me crazy but I respect it because it assures me that you are smart, strong, independent and you will be anything you want in life because you have the willpower to do it. I love you for your determination that this world will not beat you down."

Delila as a toddler smiling taking a selfie with her mom, Kristina.

Thank you to my family and friends that make me feel like I'm not alone. You helped me to become who I am today. No matter what disability you have you are still a human being, if people are judging you let them be because they'll realize they made a mistake and change. When I see other people that have similar backgrounds as me and are isolated, I feel like they don't have a voice. I encourage them to have the courage to advocate for themselves and they can do anything. That is what DEAF POWER is all about! This is why I wrote this book.

—Delila Vasquez

In CHARGE of My Life

Early Years

When I was born, my parents found out that I have a rare disorder called CHARGE Syndrome. It stands for *coloboma of the eye (looks like a keyhole), heart defects, atresia of the choanae (hard to breathe through my nose), restriction of growth and development (okay, okay, I'm short, but I'm cute), ear abnormalities and deafness.* I am Deaf, blind in my right eye and have low vision and peripheral (side) loss in my left eye. At first my parents were scared that I may not be healthy and could not hear. The combination of both hearing and vision loss is called DeafBlind.

I got my first hearing aids at three months old. I walked before I crawled. My mom says I was a well-behaved child. Sometimes I was injured because I am Deaf and have a vision impairment. I was always bumping into things or falling down. My visual impairment blocks my peripheral vision, what I can see on the side, it's okay I turn my head to see. The combination of sensory loss makes it difficult to know when I'm being spoken to unless the person is standing directly in front of me. I received Early Childhood Intervention at home. Then I went to a Deaf Education Preschool and received speech and vision services. I learned sign language and began to talk!

I was in the hospital many times and had nine surgeries. To help me hear I have a bone anchored hearing auditory implant, called a BAHA. I had a Tracheotomy and feeding tube when I was about three. I had a scary experience one time when my trach came loose, my grandma said, "It doesn't fit," and called the ambulance. They took it out while I was awake! I could feel the tools, it was very scary. I missed school for many days. I felt self-conscious and wore a jacket to hide the scar, so people wouldn't ask me about it.

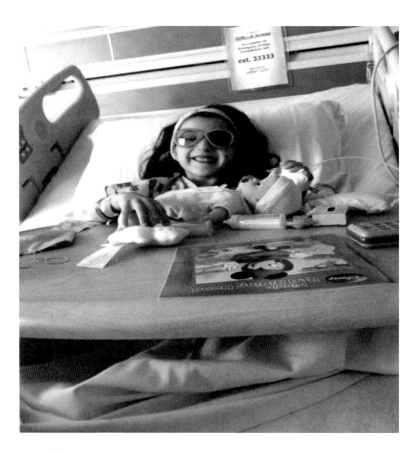

Delila smiling in a hospital bed playing with a doll.

My mom began to learn American Sign Language right away, but I was stubborn and did not like to practice with my family. Now that I'm older, I wish we signed more at home. I wanted to fit in at home, but it was hard to communicate, so I would act up. I'm the only one in my family with hearing loss. My mom said it was difficult to communicate with me. I would get so frustrated and throw things, I tried to find ways to help them understand what I wanted by pulling their hand, pointing, climbing, and sometimes crying.

I knew how to push my mom's buttons!!! I have always been a strong and independent young woman. I did mischievous things like climbing upon the counter to get candy on top of the refrigerator but also to gain knowledge or bargain with my siblings to get what I wanted.

Delila standing with her older sister and two younger brothers in front of a Christmas tree and gifts.

Elementary

Delila's school picture in 2nd Grade.

In elementary I was sassy and gave everyone a hard time, because I always felt like I was in someone else's shadow. I wanted attention. When I got in trouble, I felt like I disappointed my grandma. I always felt like I was getting picked on and things are always my fault. I remember being sad because I missed the father-daughter dance because of a surgery, but dad cheered me up by joking around and making me laugh. We watched movies and he said, when I was better, he would take me out somewhere fun.

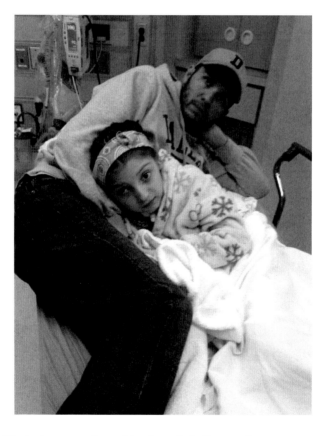

Delila being comforted by her dad, Jose, after surgery.

Many service providers work with me at school. Audiologist, Deaf Ed teachers, interpreters, vision teachers, speech pathologist, orientation and mobility specialist and counselors and many more. There are so many people on my team to help me be successful. It was harder for me to learn and read because I'm Deaf but now I am caught up and can speak, sign and read very well. This book is in large print 18 point font so I can read it clearer too! We all must know our accommodations that help us get access to learn our best.

Middle School

Starting middle school was very dramatic, I was finding my way, socializing, meeting new friends and caring too much about gossip. I had stress headaches. In the seventh grade I realized if I was going to do well in high school it was time to behave and mature. I was put in all mainstream classes and out of the security of my small Deaf Education classroom. When Covid hit and we had to learn from home I had to switch to learning on the computer.

By 8th grade I was passing all of my classes and college bound. I gained insight, maturity, and began planning for high school and college. I felt less stressed and positive! Having CHARGE syndrome used to bother me in elementary but after middle school I began to accept my disability. It takes time to feel confident and that's okay. There is no need to rush! Mental health is important for everyone, and you need to take care of yourself. I think positively and try to do something that makes me happy.

One time during a Halloween party, I had glow stick liquid splattered on me. Students were having fun breaking them and throwing the glowing liquid everywhere. I didn't know why I was so itchy! My BAHA was off so I could only communicate in sign language. I ran to the bathroom and saw spots all over me. Some girls took me to a police officer and the principal and they called my mom on Facetime because they could not communicate with me. I went to the hospital for hours and I couldn't eat because of an allergic reaction! We did not even know I was allergic to anything.

Delila in Middle School High School

High School

As a freshman I liked my new school, classes and friends. I have to be aware of my surroundings, I walk fast and talk with friends. Sometimes I bump into things and people. I have to slow down and learn protective techniques from my orientation and mobility instructor. One time in the hallway students started a fight. My back was turned and I didn't see or hear what was behind me and got knocked down.

Delila in a conversation with Seandra Reese, Deaf interpreter.

I use an interpreter in class, a video relay interpreter on the computer. I tried my best and passed Algebra and

Biology STAAR tests! It was hard. I'm very proud.

Delila watching Video Relay Interpreter during English class.

I want to go to college to be a script consultant and help others improve their writing. My transition goals focus on learning about opportunities to become an author and finding colleges that offer classes for that career.

I enjoy going to counseling, it gives me time to express how I feel and handle when I am stressed. I'm very lucky to have a Counselor that is Deaf too and can communicate with me because he really understands what it's like to be Deaf. My family and friends are important to me so I'm working on communication, social skills, and building self-esteem. I'm learning ways to handle emotions like controlling my temper by using breathing exercises, thinking happy thoughts, journaling or just walking away. Sometimes I get frustrated easily in social situations, I do not like to repeat myself when I'm not understood and say "never mind" and end up not being able to have a conversation. I'm learning if I'm not understood to explain in detail and not just repeating the word. Sometimes you have to control your feelings before you act out or do something you don't mean to. It's okay if things mess up because it will be worth it in the end. I feel released. Everybody has different ways of handling feelings, including me. You're not the only one and it's okay. It is also okay to ask for help, even if you are very stubborn. It helps me a lot and it will help you too.

Drivers Vision Test

I passed the vision exam for driving at the Low Vision Clinic. I had to pass in order to see if I would be able to be qualified to take the driver's test. I looked into a machine and clicked a button when I saw a dot on the screen. I passed! I am ready to take drivers ed. I was very nervous because I didn't think I would be able to drive because of my vision loss. I'm planning on going to the driver's class in the summer at The Texas School for the Deaf in Austin.

Quinceañera

Delila in her Quinceañera dress.

I had a fabulous Quinceañera. I prepared for months and found the most beautiful dress. When I got into my dress for my picture my heart was pounding, it felt like a dream come true. Even though it was Covid, people still came. I cried at the father daughter dance because I was so sad before when I missed it in Elementary. I felt like a princess, like I was living in a fairytale, cheerful moment of my life.

Tennis

A favorite memory for me was when I was in elementary school. I was in the tennis club with my friends who are Deaf. Every year we went on a field trip through the Dallas Tennis Association to a tennis club, T Bar M Racquet Club. We watched a professional match and the coaches gave us lesson drills. When I went to high school, I was so excited when I got on the tennis team. We warm up and take turns passing the ball. I have a school tennis uniform.

Delila about to hit a tennis ball with her racquet.

At first it was complicated, but I got the hang of it. The coach is understanding and knows, if it is raining, I can take off my BAHA during practice. People are so surprised that I play tennis because I have sight in only one eye. I can see centrally but not peripherally so, if the ball is coming at me or goes beside me, I have to turn my head to see it so I do not miss it.

Space Camp

My sophomore year I went to Space Camp in Alabama. It was an experience of a lifetime. I made many new friends who are blind from other states and countries! I taught them how to sign Space Camp words, such as rocket, airplane, space, stars and for the instruments we used during our activities. I gave my new friends sign names, which are not standard but unique to each person and given by a person who is Deaf. I showed them the signs for every country and state that was represented at camp. Some of them read braille. We keep in contact by text and email. They use a screen reader to hear what I write, but I really want to learn to read braille too.

I tried on an astronaut suit and wore it in a training activity.

Delila wearing an astronaut suit, standing on a machine that lifts her high in the air.

Camp affected me by making me feel confident and challenged with different opportunities. I learned so many things about space, it was so interesting, like the sun is not yellow or red, it's white! I never thought there was sound in space, the stars sounded like a Disney movie. Mars sounds like a scary movie, very interesting, it was so cool! I learned that the warm water in the pool feels like the temperature in space. I learned what space looks like and sounds like. We made model rockets and had fun launching them. I used a computer on a mission to speak through the microphone connected to my BAHA to communicate with people in space.

Most of all I learned that I am a leader and to help everyone. I made it to the top of the Pamper Pole, given the name because it is so tall and scary, it was hard. I took the longest time out of my group but I made it and conquered my biggest fear.

Delila smiling with her arm raised because she went up high and conquered her fear of heights.

My favorite moment was standing on the Canadarm, a robotic arm used to deploy and maneuver astronauts and cargo. I experienced facing my fear of heights and being able to look around. I felt like I was floating.

While I watched everyone graduating, at the end someone said my name out loud and I realized I won the Max Carpenter

Kathy Johnson award! It is for the camper that "exemplifies the spirit of the founders at SCIVIS and overcomes their own challenges." My perceived challenges were my fear of height and my speech. I worried my team wouldn't understand me which would impact the success of my team. I had two interpreters, and we figured it out. I was so excited and realized I affect everyone's life in a positive way. I was so overwhelmed I cried. I can't wait to tell everyone my experience and hope I can do this again. One little girl came up to me and asked what I did to win the award. I told her I wanted to show them that even though I am DeafBlind I can join in and have fun, even if it is hard for me, I still want to try. I want Deaf and blind people to do anything in the world they want to do. I want to help everyone to join opportunities and asked if Deaf students can come to Space Camp too, now they are opening it back up to students who are Deaf. It was an amazing experience.

Delila receiving her award.

When I came back home I shared my experience. I want to tell everyone in Deaf Ed so they can apply and go. They too can become interested, have fun, make new friends, have the opportunity to experience and know what it's like to be in space.

Delila's award, medal, and recommendation letter.

Advocate

What I want teachers to know is that gathering information for me takes longer, so slow down the pace of instruction. I have to overcompensate to watch the interpreter, turn my head to see the board, it is best to stand at the board if you are teaching from it. Sensory loss limits incidental learning which results in significantly less essential background information. I often experience listening fatigue which can result in stress as well as feelings of inadequacy and failure.

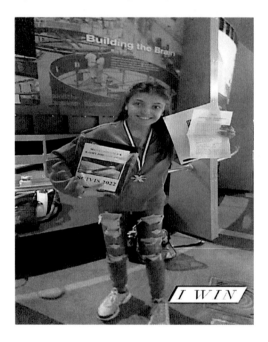

Delila holding her award, medal, and recommendation letter.

I was nervous at first but now I participate in my ARD meetings. Teachers should be open to allowing students to show them their perspective about their learning needs, accommodations, and include them in making goals.

I feel good when I inspire others. My godmother started working with infants with hearing loss because of me. It makes me feel good about myself. Finally, do what makes you happy and keep doing it! I learned that my happiness is that I love helping others and dancing.

Afterword

I have learned so much over the years as your teacher observing, making mistakes, trial and error. But thankfully, I've become a better teacher, better listener, and more understanding of the impact of DeafBlindness. I've learned that sometimes we miss out by not being in touch with other's perspectives, observing every clue. I must be open to allowing students to teach me too.

We began this project when she was in middle school as an IEP goal to learn about CHARGE Syndrome and resources state and nationwide. She wants to become a writer to inspire others to be confident and share her hope. We began working on Social Emotional activities during Covid, so she can focus on positive aspects in her life, making a timeline of events during her life, a genogram of her family, really taking an in depth look at who she is and what it feels like living with CHARGE Syndrome. All of these combined activities put into perspective the impact DeafBlindness has portrayed in her life, which became the foundation of the book. At a young age she went through behavioral issues, anger, frustration and inadequacies.

It's been such a blessing to see her become such a positive, joyful, confident and strong young lady. I have seen her meet other students that were quiet and insecure then she modeled that confidence and friendship which made them blossom.

—Crystal Sapir, Teacher of Students who are DeafBlind

What Educators Need Know When Working With Students Who Are DeafBlind

Students who are DeafBlind have to work harder than their peers to gather information and often experience fatigue. It takes longer so the pace of instruction should be slower. Students who are Deaf and have low vision have to over-compensate to watch the interpreter. It is best to stand at the board facing the class if you are teaching from it. Turning your back while continuing to speak will cause missed information. This can result in extremely high levels of stress as well as feelings of inadequacy.

Sensory loss limits or prohibits incidental learning through the student's life. This results in the child having significantly less essential background information. The scope of the information in a general education classroom can be overwhelming. Modifying and/or accommodating the curricular content prioritizes the curriculum so it is both manageable and instructive.

Made in the USA
Coppell, TX
20 September 2024

37482427R00024